DEDICATION

Dedicated especially for "TI Friend and Friend" reader ...

Your book "**Positioning your personal brand** *-Consolidate and position your PERSONAL BRANDING in a competitive market through "Love Brand" © ®"*. We provide the tools you require to begin to create, build, position and strengthen your image of personal brand through "Love Brand". And with the principles of success collected in this book you begin your process of creating, styling and build your own PERSONAL BRANDING.

And this; It is my intention, for you ...

Your Great Friend *Ylich Tarazona*

*Consolidate and Position your PERSONAL BRANDING on a
Competitive Market Through "Love Brand"*
Written by Master Coach: YLICH TARAZONA

Positioning Your Personal Brand
Written by Master Coach: YLICH TARAZONA
SERIES: Basic Principles and Introductory Succeeding Success - Volume 5 of 7

Positioning Your Personal Brand
Consolidate and Position your PERSONAL BRANDING in a Competitive Market Through "Love Brand"

Wonderful Book Self-help and personal venture that will help you **POSITIONING your personal brand** on a fantastic journey of rediscovering Professional, allowing you **HIGHLIGHT, consolidate and establish your personal branding in a competitive market through** "Love Brand" and develop the most out of your human potential to the next level, inspiring you to live an extraordinary life principle-centered.

In this book in its special edition you will learn to:

- Program your conscious and subconscious mind to professional success and personal fulfillment.
- Allow optimal configuration beliefs, and empower your ability to create and build your personal brand IMAGE through both face and virtual strategies ONLINE OFFLINE
- Promote flexibility of tactical thinking - strategic and understanding of mental and psychological processes to position your "personal brand" in your circle of influence through "Love Brand".
- Having an action plan and a draft clear and well-defined life that allows you to build your PERSONAL BRANDING.
- Re-discover your mission and purpose of life and understand the reasons why it is important to establish your own personal brand.
- Know and master the basic principles of CEREBRAL Reengineering and the mental programming that allow you to take action, make things happen, and start living an extraordinary life centered on principles that inspire you to establish your IMAGE personal brand through " Love Brand ".

3rd Revised Edition, Updated and Extended
(Includes exercises and Plan of Action)

Transformational Coach

Writer and lecturer International

*Consolidate and Position your PERSONAL BRANDING on a
Competitive Market Through "Love Brand"*
Written by Master Coach: YLICH TARAZONA

3rd Special Edition *Revised and Updated by:* ***Ylich Tarazona*** *October 2017.
Design and Preparation of the Cover by: Ylich Tarazona*

ISBN-13: **978-1979861687** *(CreateSpace-Assigned)*
ISBN-10: **1979861684** *(CreateSpace-Assigned)*
STAMP*: Independently Published* ©

BISAC: Personal Brand / Personal Branding / Love Brand / Entrepreneurship
The right of **YLICH TARAZONA** *to be identified as the* **AUTHOR** *of this work has been affirmed by SafeCreative.org, Registration Code:* **1711184869558***, in accordance with* **Copyright Worldwide***. Date:* **November 17, 2017***.*

COPYRIGHT

This book in its special edition called "*Positioning your personal brand - Consolidate and position your PERSONAL BRANDING in a competitive market through "Love Brand"* © ®". Applied to strategies - Self-Help, Motivation, Personal Redesign, Entrepreneurship, Personal Brand or Personal Branding, "Love Brand" and Neuro - Coaching for setting goals and achievements of objectives through the "neurolinguistics programming IMPLEMENTED" is the intellectual property of YLICH TARAZONA © & Mental Reengineering with NLP ®.

FOLLOW THROUGH OUR OFFICIAL WEBSITE
http://www.reingenieriamentalconpnl.com

LEGAL WARNING: Copyright © November 2017 by YLICH TARAZONA ® & Reengineering WITH MENTAL PNL ®. All Rights Reserved Worldwide ©. No part of this book personal brand may be stored in system data recovery, or may be reproduced or modified partial or full mode, similarly also can be reduced, enlarged or transmitted in any manner or by any other format or medium, either electronic, digital copy, virtual, mechanical or manual printing. Including photocopying, scanning, recording, reproduction and distribution via online, oral or written, or any other storage system information, public or private communication and software data recovery for commercial use or profit without warning or permission in writing to the Editor, the author, and its legal representative. Those who violate these rules will be severely punished according to the laws of copyright and copyright.

YLICH TARAZONA the right to be identified as the author of this work has been affirmed by SafeCreative.org, Registration *Code:* **1711184869558**, *in accordance with **Copyright Worldwide**. Date:* **November 17, 2017.**

EDITOR'S NOTES: It is totally forbidden to use our products for commercial or for-profit, except for purposes of your own personal and professional development, and we understand that: You can use this product as a reference for their own therapy sessions and implementation techniques for personal use and always when in accordance with the lawful and legal realization of acceptable practices and ethics.

Legal assistance:
LAWYER: Mariam Charytin Murillo Velazco
CI: V-17502580, - INPREABOGADO: No. 158611

Consolidate and Position your PERSONAL BRANDING on a
Competitive Market Through "Love Brand"

Written by Master Coach: YLICH TARAZONA

MENTAL REENGINEERING NLP It is a virtual community for entrepreneurs. One of the Internet Website dedicated to providing COACHING in consolidating Skills and Development of Human Potential Maximum. Specialists in training, education and training of high level through NLP or Neuro Linguistic Programming, specializing in the supply of training and courses to achieve goals, objectives and consolidate effective Flesh results optimal performance; through a series of books, EBook's, Audios, Podcasters, Tele-Seminars Online, Audio-Visual Workshops, Webinars and Conferences Master of attending classes.

You cannot pretend to be associated with YLICH TARAZONA & MENTAL reengineering PNL in any form or use our name in connection with your own personal or professional practice, unless you are properly trained and certified validates that it proves that formally trained, properly trained or trained with us.

3rd Special Edition *Revised and Updated by:* **Ylich Tarazona** *October 2017.*
Design and Preparation of the Cover by: Ylich Tarazona

ISBN-13: **978-1979861687** *(CreateSpace-Assigned)*
ISBN-10: **1979861684** *(CreateSpace-Assigned)*
STAMP: Independently Published ©

BISAC: Personal Brand / Personal Branding / Love Brand / Entrepreneurship
The right of **YLICH TARAZONA** to be identified as the **AUTHOR** of this work has been affirmed by SafeCreative.org, Registration Code: **1711184869558**, in accordance with **Copyright Worldwide**. Date: **November 17, 2017.**

CONTRIBUTORS:
Mariam Charytin Murillo Velazco
Ylich Leavitt Gabriel Peña Smith Tarazona
Jeffry Samuel Peña Tarazona
Genesis Zarahemla Odaylich Tarazona Maldonado

If this book of personal brand in its special edition has been of interest and want us to keep you informed of our upcoming publications, editions, mini courses, special reports, video conferences, webinars, online and offline seminars, audio books, podcasters or our online services offline as sessions, coaching, therapies, corporate events, courses, workshops, seminars, conferences and other activities classroom or instructional materials designed and created by the author & MENTAL reengineering PNL; write to us, telling us what topics are of interest and we will gladly keep you updated.

You can also contact the author directly via e-mail by:
MásterCoach.YlichTarazona@gmail.com

INTRODUCTION
Relevant information for this edition.

Hello such, my dear readers. First of all, thanks for purchasing this extraordinary book of Personal Brand, I wrote thinking of you.

Before we begin, I want to communicate some essential changes I have made in this 3rd Special Edition. If you have some of my previous versions; You will see that I have made some revisions and important updates in the latest editions, as I seemed necessary to achieve fulfill the purpose for which I wrote this book for you. Among the changes I have made, I have incorporated a number of examples and practical exercises related to the lesson of some of the most relevant chapters. In the few cases where edit the text or change some content, they have been to adapt better examples and exercises recently incorporated in the present work.

These changes are almost imperceptible in most cases, since first of all I wanted to respect the original manuscript and the main idea of this book with its flaws and virtues. So, in the few occasions when I have incorporated some ideas, I've added some extra point or I added some elements of interest to my readers and learners, it is because I found convenient or necessary and vital to the proper application the principles of "Personal Reinvention, Mental bioprogramming, **Human Brain Process Reengineering, Entrepreneurship, Personal Brand** or Personal Branding and **Love Brand**" Contained in this special edition.

> *If you had the opportunity to read some of my other printed or digital books, you have seen that both the literary style of my writing; and typographic characteristic style that I use when translating my ideas, seek a single purpose. Help you develop your full human potential to the next level, and allow a better understanding of the concepts, definitions and action plan that I share with all of you in order to help them internalize these vital and essential principles to your own life.*

To achieve this goal; at the end of some key chapters, I share a range of exercises that allow you to implement the essence of what you just studied. Likewise, I also offer them a series of summations or to reflect basic principles that will help you reinforce what you've learned.

Thus, champions and champions at the end of the book you will have real strategies, techniques, tools and effective methodologies that have been studied and tested over the years by the greatest experts in the field. Likewise, these principles have been implemented and put into action again and again by the same author, both personally and in their sections of coaching and both virtual lectures and face, with hundreds and thousands of people who they have applied these principles to their own lives effectively.

Such procedures have been routinely incorporated into this book to guarantee optimal results by MODELS effective NLP or NLP APPLIED and CEREBRAL reengineering have been checked through the years by the most renowned expert's history. Thus, avoiding the use of guesswork or simple theories.

> For this reason, APPRENTICE and dear readers, I'll give you some advice: Connect with the essence of this book, ACTIVELY LEE, every word, every line, every paragraph, every page, every chapter, every idea, every teaching, every example, every story, every exercise, every principle that love with all of you, and see how; gradually, step by step, line by line and precept upon precepts begin to have the excellent results required in each and every one of the most important and essential aspects of his life.

This book is my dear readers is a powerful theoretical and practical for those who want to learn to develop their maximum human potential tool. Of course, this book is not the only means for your emotional release. However, if you follow the directions step by step I in this book, and have the right attitude and the confidence, determination and commitment can assure you apply these principles to your own personal life.

> It is important to note at this point that the Universal Laws of Success you'll learn in this book involve a lot of responsibility. Always keep in mind that the correct application of these basic principles to succeed and these universal laws of success can be properly used to come into harmony with the universal divine source. That is what ultimately allow us to generate those great and extraordinary mental and emotional changes both in our inner self and your inner self. With this in mind, I want you to understand that this book gives you the basics needed to succeed together with the Law and Universal Principles so as to ensure both your own well-being; like all those around you. The use you give you will depend on your choice,

YOU IMAGINE all you can accomplish get to learn apply these universal laws of success in your own life. You can imagine how your life would change dramatically for the better, to be able to conquer all fondest your dreams, goals and objectives you set out to achieve in this life, thanks to these **basic principles for success.** NOW POSSIBLE!

LITERARY AND MY STYLE WORKS TYPOGRAPHIC

The teachings containing my books and courses mostly, are a strategic combination mixed with powerful metaphors, parables, allegories, illustrations, stories, quotes and quotations that have been collecting and summarizing during the years from different sources; such as books and works of various authors (to which, granted them all the credit and recognition they deserve for their valuable contributions).

The objective of extracting extraordinary collection of these great and renowned writers and translate them into my works is; help them better understand my readers, I want to convey information subjectively. In this way; through learning of symbolic and figurative representations, you my friends to acquire the main ideas.

So; my books, through their quotes, famous quotes, thoughts, stories, reflections and illustrative narratives can become a source of inspiration to help those individuals with full purpose of heart they want to change and transform their lives continuously and permanently.

Another of the Typographical I use to write my work methodologies; It is to use different literary styles, introducing a variety of punctuation, bold, italic, underlined, letter case combinations, among other conscious repetitions of ideas and teachings transmitted several times; again, and again, but in different contexts and situations, to record them in your conscious and subconscious mind. As well as sometimes "strategically change the way you write and express my ideas intentionally first, second and third person" lie I transmit information, in order to make the most didactic, versatile and pleasant reading for all my readers.

Should this seem inappropriate or wrong at some point for some of my readers, I want anticipate them in advance that it is not in any way an oversight on my part, or lack of editing and transcription of the work. On the contrary, it has a clear objective and pursues a particular purpose. TRUST ME. It has a purpose for you, keep reading and you'll understand what I mean.

In another order of idea; Importantly also incorporated in the course of the book a wide variety of famous quotes, inspirational quotes scripture, Bible verses, philosophical concepts, examples, similes, exhibitions, descriptions and figured in the course of the whole work language. Since such expressions, concepts and ideas are able to subjectively stimulate a variety of sensations MULTI-SENSORY at both (visual, auditory and kinesthetic) that allow evoke images, sounds, sensations and emotions in the reader's mind.

Consolidate and Position your PERSONAL BRANDING on a
Competitive Market Through "Love Brand"

Written by Master Coach: YLICH TARAZONA

Following the same order of idea; I include in all my works a series of positive statements, self-statements empowering, based on META-MODELS strategic NLP through a series of hypnotic commands and persuasive patterns that allow the reader to incorporate these suggestions and Subliminal inductions your mind conscious and subconscious, and producing them radically positive changes in their mental and psychological structure, creating in new neural connections more empowering.

And finally, APPRENTICE, among other resources I use are personal expressions like you and IT, to refer directly to my readers, with the sole intention that they can feel identified with my words, and have the full assurance and conviction that all I write my books thinking about them.

In the audible versions, such as in cases of audiobooks, podcasters, the Webminars, the Tele-Seminars and Online Conferences I use instrumental background music with sounds of nature, and at times binaural waves at different frequencies. To induce certain positive states in the brain. Among the many benefits offered by these powerful tools it is conducive to accelerated learning, conscious reflection, proper assimilation of ideas, mental alertness, stimulation of creativity, relaxation, concentration and meditation among many other advantages. As they have shown in numerous studies on the subject. Including the doctoral thesis <u>Pedro Miguel González Velasco PhD in Neuroscience from the Completeness University of Madrid FACULTY OF PSYCHOLOGY</u>, Which we report excellent and wonderful positive effects of these sounds, both psychological and physiological.

The purpose of introducing this range of literary, typographic styles; METAPHORICAL and binaural (the latter only in cases Audible), merged with a varied set of techniques NLP or Neuro Linguistic Programming Applied Reengineering Principles Cerebral Neuro-Coaching autohypnosis among other tools. It is to enable my readers receive a transformational education more useful, holistic and comprehensive, enabling them to embrace new ideas, thus avoiding the slightest resistance to change, and creating a greater psychological impact - emotional in the retention process - learning.

******IMPORTANT******

This book in its special edition is a transcription adapted from Podcasters, Webminars, teleseminar, online course and face-offline Conference Coach entitled Ylich Tarazona "Positioning your personal brand -**Consolidate and position your PERSONAL BRANDING in a competitive market through "Love Brand" © ®"**. For that reason; this book reflects a unique and original style of transcription. Since it is an adaptation of a work Audio and Video Course Conference; rather than a literary work, written as such.

TABLE OF CONTENTS

COPYRIGHT AND COPYRIGHT .... - 3 -
DEDICATION .... - 5 -
INTRODUCTION .... - 7 -
   Relevant information for this edition. .... - 7 -
LITERARY AND MY STYLE WORKS TYPOGRAPHIC .... - 9 -
   ******IMPORTANT****** .... - 10 -
TABLE OF CONTENTS .... - 11 -
CHAPTER I PERSONAL BRANDING OR PERSONAL MARK .... - 12 -
   PART ONE: INTRODUCTION TO PERSONAL BRANDING .... - 12 -
   PART TWO: WHY must create, POSITIONING AND BUILD YOUR PERSONAL OR PERSONAL BRANDING BRAND? .... - 14 -
   PART THREE: HOW IMPORTANT IS THE PERSONAL BRAND .... - 16 -
   PART FOUR: PERSONAL BRANDING or personal brand ONLINE .... - 18 -
   WHY OUR POSITION "PERSONAL BRANDING" or "Personal Brand" on the Internet? .... - 18 -
   WHY DISCLOSE your personal brand INTERNET .... - 19 -
   PART FIVE: TE TE EXTINGUES distinguish O: Your PERSONAL BRAND HAS TO DIFFER FROM THE REST. .... - 22 -
   PART SIX: Creating and build your personal brand IMAGE OR PERSONAL BRANDING .... - 24 -
   Tips for positioning your personal brand strategies in person OFFLINE ....- 27 -
   How to create a strategy of "LOVE BRAND". .... - 33 -
   Elements must have a good strategy "LOVE BRAND" for positioning and consolidate your brand. .... - 34 -
WORKBOOK .... - 35 -
   DETERMINE YOUR PLAN OF ACTION, positioning your personal brand ....- 35 -
FINAL WORDS .... - 41 -
ABOUT THE AUTHOR .... - 43 -
OTHER PUBLICATIONS, SPECIAL EDITIONS, MINI COURSES, BOOKS E-BOOK'SY by the author .... **¡Error! Marcador no definido.**
FOLLOW THROUGH ALL OUR NETWORKS SOCIAL (SOCIAL MEDIA AND OFFICIAL WEBSITE) .... **¡Error! Marcador no definido.**

Consolidate and Position your PERSONAL BRANDING on a Competitive Market Through "Love Brand"

Written by Master Coach: YLICH TARAZONA

CHAPTER I PERSONAL BRANDING OR PERSONAL MARK

PART ONE: INTRODUCTION TO PERSONAL BRANDING

Hello such, champions and champions, a big hello. This time I will share with you about an issue that has been evolving over the years and has now had much boom in different sectors. Considered by some experts as one of the most important points for entrepreneurship in the XXI century. PERSONAL BRANDING or personal branding is a concept that has been strengthened over time by which certain people consider as which DISTINCTIVE BRAND ORIGINAL such as a trade mark would consider Acknowledged. And this process, aims, let us know unique, exclusive and innovative way that allows us to differentiate ourselves from the rest, transmit our essence, and to achieve the greatest possible impact on both our personal relationships,

> Personal branding perspective is obtained through perception, vision, and the idea that others differ from us. That is, the personal branding becomes an intangible asset that includes our image, we radiate outward appearance, the positive impression that we cause, we convey the qualities and personal magnetism or influence we have on others; in the same way, as would cast large commercial Brands.
>
> For this reason, personal branding has as main purpose the impression that we cause in people is effective, efficient and permanent in time. It is for this reason that personal branding is a powerful tool that allows us to apply the same knowledge, procedures, tactics and strategies used by commercial brand, but in this case, to ourselves.

Today we live in the concept of personal branding or PERSONAL BRANDING, it becomes increasingly necessary and indispensable to make a difference and leave a mark in this competitive globalized era. In which only those who excel will be those most likely to succeed. To consolidate the above idea, we can add that personal brand or personal branding is the way we have to position ourselves, consolidate and make ourselves known to ourselves. That is, that this has to become an extension of who we are, inside and outside our circle of influence, either personally and professionally.

> PERSONAL BRAND you must be identified by what you offer the world; either through your skills, your business skills, personal skills you possess in different areas of your life and artistic talents that distinguish you from the rest of others.
>
> PERSONAL BRANDING You have to be recognized for the added value you bring to others, you have the capabilities and allow you to help and serve a certain group of people in a specific need with these unique gifts that you possess.

Your personal brand will be the track that you let MARKED on all individuals who come in contact with daily. Those who know you, who follow your path, you are within your circle of social influence possibly friends, family, acquaintances, future prospects, customers, partners, supporters and an infinite chain of unlimited opportunities that will open due to CREATE AROUND IT, an image, a product, a service or a need that only you can PROVIDE. For me personally, this is one of the best definitions I have found to describe generally, while representing simple PERSONAL BRANDING.

To complete this concept, I will share with you the opinion that reinforces the main idea I want to teach in this chapter. TOM PETERS recognized American author in an article published in "The Brand called you" that appeared in the magazine "Fast Company" in August 1997 stated that: "The only way to differentiate ourselves from the rest in an increasingly competitive world is driving our careers as large companies manage their product brands. "

> Remember think, feel and act like the person you want to be, until you are. "{(Keep in mind that start SHAPING a winning attitude and end with building a winning PERSONALITY)}". -. YLICH TARAZONA. -

"I firmly believe that there is within the interior of each of us a seed of greatness, lies a vast reservoir of unlimited potential and usually remain dormant skills; waiting to be discovered, developed and exploited, to blossom into our outer world. When each of us awaken the individual potential, we rediscover what our mission and purpose that gives meaning to our lives, we will open the way to a new awakening conscious what I call reinventing and reengineering PERSONAL "-. YLICH TARAZONA. -

*Consolidate and Position your PERSONAL BRANDING on a
Competitive Market Through "Love Brand"*
Written by Master Coach: YLICH TARAZONA

PART TWO: WHY must create, POSITIONING AND BUILD YOUR PERSONAL OR PERSONAL BRANDING BRAND?

One reason, champions and champions why we must create, position and strengthen our image Personal Brand or Personal Branding is because we are living in the Age of Digital Guy, the Age of globalized people, where your friend and my friend You are the most important. But to achieve this goal, you have to make yourself known as a person and professional, in other words, YOU HAVE BECOME THE BEST OF IT VERSION THEREOF that allows you to position yourself in your niche, what you like and you know do well.

It is impossible to create, position and strengthen your image Personal Brand Personal Branding or being an expert on the sly, or a stranger in a highly competitive business world. You must stop being an expert only at home, where possibly the only place where you know you're good at this or any subject, or good at doing this or anything. Today to let you know, you should dare to step out of your comfort zone, which is where possibly only your friends, neighbors, colleagues, relatives and acquaintances know your skills. They already know, NOW THE TIME HAS COME IN WHICH THE WHOLE WORLD MUST ALSO KNOW.

You cannot go with so much talent in the dark. You have to let you know, that means you have to bring to light what identifies you and makes you unique and special. If you do not give to know, you're staying out of the game. If ever happened to your head that you do not have talent, you are completely wrong, as we all have to some extent gifts, talents, abilities, virtues, skills and competences in which we excel in certain activities. And the purpose of this mini course and report on its special edition is to help you rediscover and recognize that natural talent and make it known to the world.

> Years ago, there was talk of the globalization of countries, today it is giving globalization, but of talent and skills, where those who manage to create, position and consolidate its image Personal Brand or Personal Branding are those who are at the forefront different market niches.

Today you are competing, no longer between companies but between a wide variety of skills, talents and skills, where future prospects and prospects wonder how you all going to help? What you offer them different from the rest of your competition? Because you have to choose you rather than others? And that, champions and champions is the dynamic that exists today. And those who have the answers to these questions and learn to create, position and consolidate its image Personal Brand or Personal Branding are the ones who are most likely to succeed in this competitive world ... And this knowledge you are receiving is the difference that makes THE DIFFERENCE, and finally it allows you to make yourself known to the world once and for all.

You have to understand, that, thanks to the digital age and globalization of talents, is making the overnight lot of companies begin to lose their power, and that power is going to individuals who have the knowledge capital and they know how to strategically launch their powers and this is where the PICTURE MARK PERSONAL BRANDING or PERSONAL comes into play.

> You are worth GOLD friend and my friend, you IMAGE OF PERSONAL BRANDING personal brand or worth millions of dollars. Maybe you're thinking, but how it is that my personal brand image is worth millions, yes, it is, because you unique, exclusive and special you are. And you, and only you do and you're the only one who can do things like only you know how. Do you understand the idea, right?

Today the Independent Business and visionary entrepreneur like you, is the protagonist. You are the actor and lead actress, you are the center, you are your own business, you create, you position yourself and consolidated own personal brand image or personal branding and decide what to do, how to do and when to do it.

You, and you alone have the responsibility of your income, finance and economics, your wellness, style and quality of life, your holiday, recreation and your time. You, and you alone who choose to offer your services, you choose to join your team, finally, you have total and absolute control of your life, you just have to believe it, take action and make things happen.

REMEMBER: "Success is not a one-day event, it is a continuous process that is repeated all life. You can be a winner in his life if he tries. BECAUSE YOU ARE A WINNER born and from the moment of conception ...

Remember: Successful people engage in activities that allow them to win from time to time; because they know that both the triumph, victory and conquest are habits that should constantly develop in your lifestyle ...

Successful people; Also, they keep in mind that it is also losing wins. Because they know that every failure brings them closer to their purpose and that every defeat strengthens and teaches them what to improve. In After; both triumphs and defeats, are so important to success, learn from them when we become stronger and worthy of living that style and extraordinary quality of life for which we have both strive day after day "-. YLICH TARAZONA. -

PART THREE: HOW IMPORTANT IS THE PERSONAL BRAND

There are a number of reasons why it is important to create and build your own personal brand.

Then I will highlight the highlights that allows us to achieve our image position publicly to develop excellent PERSONAL BRANDING. As this gives us the opportunity to quasar a strong impact around our professional status. Some of the most important reasons are:

1. A strong personal brand and well-established makes creating a business or entrepreneurship a "micro-enterprise staff" more feasible.

2. A personal brand you become more visible in society, opens the doors before a more competitive world, because you can make yourself known as an expert in a given area.

3. A personal brand allows you to generate greater credibility, trust and security before potential customers, prospects, partner, employers, investors or interested in the goods, services or products you offer around the image you have created around you.

4. A personal brand gives you the opportunity to position yourself in your field of excellence, allowing more easily focus on the issues that you love. Resulting in higher quality goods, services or products that offer the global market.

5. A personal brand you favor when selling because it gives you the privilege of charging better prices for your goods, services or products. Since having created a well-established tea image becomes a trademark request.

> "I never said it easy, but I promise you it will not be impossible ... You just have to be willing to pay the price of success and then enjoy the results the rest of his entire life." - YLICH TARAZONA. -

PART FOUR: PERSONAL BRANDING or personal brand ONLINE

WHY OUR POSITION "PERSONAL BRANDING" or "Personal Brand" on the Internet?

With the advent of virtual world, the fact of creating a career in INTERNE is paramount and essential for anyone. As recently proved; according to recent studies and statistics conducted on the subject. It has been shown that 80% of the population around the world already use the internet for various technological means as an option or alternative for different uses such as:

- Find or offer job via online.
- Search professional candidates for a job
- Get future, customers, prospects, partners or businesses.
- Buy, sell and market goods, services or products.
- Create profiles on some of the most popular social networks.
- Search, upload or download information on topics of interest.
- **Navigate the different options available on the web find.** Anyway; We could list a lot of viable reasons to why the world of cyberspace is useful today for an infinite number of opportunities, but this is not the main theme of the chapter.

Good champions and champions, once the previous section continue with the subject that interests us is the importance of the position of our personal brand online clarified.

> BRAND PERSONAL virtual path; is just let us know so massively online on the internet to position our image as a watermark. For this purpose, it is necessary to apply certain tactics and marketing strategies to highlight and publicize our natural talents, skills, abilities, skills or experiences you have in a specific area that allows us to project as an expert in the field.

Another benefit offered by the position yourself as a personal brand online is that it allows you to announce your greatest strengths, take a clear and convincing your audience how you can help you solve this or that challenge, obstacle or adversity message so they can advance to the next level in your life purpose, at the same time know you are going CONSOLIDATING your own dreams, goals, objectives.

Positioning Your Personal Brand
Written by Master Coach: YLICH TARAZONA

PERSONAL BRANDING you or PERSONAL BRAND also it gives you the opportunity to be present in the minds of your customers or prospects as a first choice when they need a suitable person to help them resolve a matter through what you offer can give you one solution.

** _ ** _ ** _ ** _ ** _ ** _ ** _ ** _ ** _ ** _ ** _ ** _ * _ * _ * _ * _ * _ * _ * _ * _ * _ * _ *
_ * _ * _ * _ * _ * _ *

WHAT distinguishes the winners from the losers?

"Winners are concentrated at all times what they know they can do well, talents, strengths, skills, abilities and skills. Although they recognize they have weaknesses; They never focus on them, but working on them ...

While the losers are scattered thinking about all those things when they do not want to do evil; focusing on their weaknesses, limitations and lack of talent, but they know they have strengths, it seems to never realize them ...

If you're good at persuading selling or communicating, then focus on those potentialities and weaknesses will become stronger as you work on them slowly, leaving aside those things where you know you're really good ... Here lies the great difference that makes the difference between winners and losers, how to act before adversity. "- YLICH TARAZONA. -

WHY DISCLOSE your personal brand INTERNET?

Understanding the processes and changes that are happening around the world, our Latin American society, need to have more entrepreneurs, Hispanic leaders and successful entrepreneurs in different professional fields that provide various alternatives in different areas of being, knowledge, personal development and self-help, as well as in the fields of business, entrepreneurship, education and financial literacy, the art of creating wealth, abundance and prosperity, other options that would also be of great value to society are issues related to values , moral principles, marriage, family, home, children, Finally there are so many markets that require influencers with special competence that through their contributions favoring users seeking guidance, mentoring orientation, being excellent candidates those with skills in coaching, neurolinguistics programming, cerebral reengineering between many other disciplines.

This is where your personal BRANDING ONLINE or personal branding comes into play and is vitally important, because they always need more experienced leaders who are generating solutions.

*Consolidate and Position your PERSONAL BRANDING on a
Competitive Market Through "Love Brand"*
Written by Master Coach: YLICH TARAZONA

And through the Internet as a medium, it is an excellent vehicle to reach literally thousands and millions of people from around the world that require your skills and competencies.

> One of the most effective ways we have to carry our message and promote our values massively in "{(INTERNET)}" is through a personal mark with "{(ONLINE PRESENCE)}". To enable us to position ourselves as leaders INFLUENTIAL AS EMPLOYERS SUCCEED AS ENTREPRENEURS high performance as experts in a particular area. And all this can be achieved if we create and build AN IMAGE well established that we become literally a "{(trademark)}" requested in the minds of thousands and millions of virtual users that "{(surfing the Web)} ".

One of the most important to create, build, consolidate and establish your own personal brand recommendations are as follows:

I.   It is authentic, original, unique and exclusive. Never try to imitate anyone; Be yourself, let see your feelings, thoughts and ideals. Inspires others through your own success story. Maybe at the beginning you need to take a person as a model, an example to follow, as a source of inspiration in what you set out. All this applies to the beginning of your training process and positioning; but once Hallas modeling patterns of excellence of this or that person, and begin to have your own experiences and results. From there onwards he begins to make your mark, to differentiate your brand and staff.

II.   Your tactics and strategies personal brand must always be accompanied by your principles and values, because they are your principles and your values that you will maintain "{(POSITIONED)}" in the minds of those who begin to believe and trust TI, and this is ultimately what will differentiate you as a reliable person.

III.   Never try to create your personal brand forged a lie or deception, because these dishonest acts discredit any result you can achieve. It is better to start gradually from scratch, perhaps from scratch, but if you have a cause you conquer your purpose.

"Success is the result of integrity and honesty in all our actions"
-. YLICH TARAZONA. -

*Consolidate and Position your PERSONAL BRANDING on a
Competitive Market Through "Love Brand"*
Written by Master Coach: YLICH TARAZONA

PART FIVE: YOU DIFFERENCES FROM OTHERS OR YOU EXTINGUISH: YOUR PERSONAL BRAND IMAGE MUST BE DIFFERENTIATED FROM THE REST.

As we have learned so far, the Internet in this globalized and digital world has made emerging countries entering the game, has made the less fortunate markets come into play, it has made the brightest come into play, has fact that the mega global corporations into play, has made considered minorities in societies entering the game, has made less valid entering the game, has made the most fortunate comes into play, it has made more prominent and competent comes into play ... and finally, if I'm not finished. I want to give you to understand is that there is today OPPORTUNITIES FOR ALL EQUALLY, or that the Internet has become a real opportunity where there is, or there are barriers to entry, and virtually all have and can be,

Now, I want you to pay full attention. As there are no barriers to entry on the Internet, therefore you have to learn to differentiate yourself from the crowd. Include this phrase I read in a Personal Branding thesis was presented in Madrid - Spain and says: "You distinguish you or you extinguish".

As we appreciate the motto "You distinguish you or you extinguish" You definitely have to learn how to create, highlight, consolidate and establish your personal brand or IMAGE OF PERSONAL BRANDING differently, only exclusive and special. It is easy to create, highlight, consolidate and position your image of personal brand or personal branding making it different from the rest of others, if you keep your essence, and you're still yourself, but giving to the world a new and improved version of yourself. If you can find your essence, be yourself, but also create a new and improved version of you be more extraordinary, your personal brand will be different, because we are unique beings, and there never will be one like us, because we are all different and talented, some are brilliant in some other activities and other activities.

And this is the difference that makes the difference, as we understand it, our life begins to make sense, because we begin to understand clearly who we are.

"I firmly believe that there is within the interior of each of us a seed of greatness and lies a vast reservoir of unlimited potential and usually remain dormant skills; waiting to be discovered and developed, to blossom into our outer world. When each of us awaken the individual potential, we rediscover what our mission and purpose that gives meaning to our lives, we will open the way to a new awakening conscious what I call reinventing and reengineering PERSONAL "
-. YLICH TARAZONA. -

Positioning Your Personal Brand
Written by Master Coach: YLICH TARAZONA

PART SIX: Creating and build your personal brand IMAGE OR PERSONAL BRANDING

Creating and building our own image of "personal brand" may seem simple at first, but actually comprises a process, and requires a few steps to achieve the expected result.

The good news champions and champions, is that there are effective ways to do so. And that's what I'll share with you below.

> To create and build an image of effective personal brand; de must positions ourselves through the appropriate channels, such as social networks, including the most recommended are Facebook, Twitter, YouTube, Google+, Blogger, LinkedIn, Instagram and many other options the most popular existing in network. Use these free platforms in our favor is one of the most effective way we have excellent benefits for short, medium and long term.
>
> By using these tools, it is important to note that our PERSONAL BRANDING have to awaken in people positive emotions that inspire you the desire to "{(TAKE ACTION)}", that is to follow, to be interested in checking your professional profile, follow your tweets, posts on your wall, you read articles on blogger, view your photos or watch your videos. Since all these activities generate WEB TRAFFIC, which is favorable in your process of building your brand PERSONAL ONLINE.
>
> The important thing is that the marketing tactics and strategies you use; allow you to be perceived social media as an alternative that can generate positive results to the needs of users require.
>
> And you can feel that you can PROVIDE THEM through what you represent or what you offer.

So that you achieve this goal I invite you to be able to take into account the following recommendations

A. Know yourself *Before creating your own personal brand must believe in you, in your potential, you can become, you must learn to know yourself, understand what you are passionate about, that's what inspires you, that is what motivates you, what you like to do, what if you do for the rest of your life would make you the happiest person in the world, understand what you want to achieve, have a clear vision of your mission purpose in life, know that you're good, you know what differences from the rest of other people, have a clear idea of what competencies, skills, gifts and talents with which accounts are. By having these conscious ideas in your mind, you can begin to build the puzzle of your success, which in this case represents your personal BRANDING.*

B. DEVELOP LOVE BRAND: *Which is a marketing concept applied to PERSONAL BRANDING has revolutionized the way how we project in our environment and circle of influence, and that turns out to be essential at the time to position and consolidate our personal brand. "Today our BRAND IMAGE OF PERSONAL need an incentive, something that differentiates us from the pile. Of those thousands of leaders and entrepreneurs like us they offer a solution to a common problem. " And the only way we have to stand before them all, is through the "Love Brand". Therefore, a "LOVE BRAND" is defined as MARCA we love. And to achieve that goal, we must remember that what drives human beings are emotion rather than reason itself. So, if we learn to win the hearts of individuals, we also earn your loyalty to our brand. Our aim should be to make him feel that our brand makes them feel happy, experiencing positive emotions, and desire inside us because we prefer us that "something" that comes to your mind as much as his heart. That is, because we have that "something" that fills them, and of which the others lack.*

C. NICHE TO KNOW YOU: *To position your brand PERSONAL most effectively and how efficiently as possible, the first thing to do is to know and understand what your niche market, ie you know what area of the market you want to reach, what kind of people, customers or prospects want to attract. Once accounts have these features must focus all your efforts to position yourself in that branch you selected. Having made this decision, you should start to train you, prepare, specialize, gain experience and begin to make yourself known as an expert in the field you have selected beforehand. Remember that the more narrow and specialized niche is you; It will be much easier to position, differentiate yourself from the rest and to stand out from others.*

D. Know what your goal: The next step is key in this process of positioning of your "personal brand". The first thing to do is define what your goals are. Once you've gone through the first three principles know yourself, DEVELOP LOVE BRAND and know your niche market, it lets you enjoy and a clearer idea of what you want, why you want it and above all already know which it is the purpose you want to achieve. Your goal might be to position yourself as an expert in international gastronomy, the art of public speaking, coaching high size, interior decorators, and manage time effectively, how to beautify your home at low cost, and achieve your goals efficiently, as finding business opportunities online, and starting a business multilevel, 7 Ways to lose weight in 30 days, in short, these are just some examples of goals. - Once you choose which will be the topic that you want to develop processes start positioning your personal brand. - "(for example, if your goal is to teach people how to improve their health and fitness -." This will be your "Now how can we break down this idea steps to help you create a plan of action. - One way would be to use the 7 ways to lose weight in 30 days since this would be an excellent choice to start, because it is in harmony with what we want, that will motivate us to offer expertise Becoming the area of welfare. and health in your niche, having purpose - "this will be you because" helping and advising people to improve their quality of life, - Then your personal goal should be to specialize in the field, to be more effective, also could be in your ideal size and speak properly and be an example of healthy lifestyle weight. - your professional goal might be: Writing eBook's, making videos, giving talks related to the issue, advise with a doctor in nutrition and dietetics, look for a sports coach you some advice, and finally let you know, and positional your personal brand the next 6 months from the next 15 working days after finding your purpose and as you create your platform on the web and social networks) ".

E. **POSITION AS OUR NAME BRAND PERSONAL** This step is already higher level, so this time we have completed the first 4 principles KNOW YOURSELF, LOVE TO DEVELOP BRAND, know your niche market and know which is your goal. - Once we have consolidated the previous 4 principles POSITIONING process begins NAME. It is the way by which you create and name for your brand that can be your own personal name, for example, is constructed: Doctor Carlos Ramírez - Leadership with Teresa Pérez, or the name of your product, goods or services you want to offer, for example: Optimum Health - Leaders with attitude, these ideas are just by placing some examples of model. - It is necessary that the name we give to our brand is effective, attractive and persuasive at the time of positioning. For that to be achieved, it is essential that our name AWAKEN EMOTIONS, FEELINGS, CURIOSITY, especially DESIRE OF WANTING TO KNOW PUBLIC. - We get our name is unique, different exclusive, short course that is pronounceable, easy to remember, especially if it could be related to what we do or the features we offer would be more commercial and of interest to others.

F. **CREATING ONLINE OPERATIONS CENTER** This point is essential if you want to have virtual presence and "{(your brand on the Internet)}" enjoy all options and unlimited benefits offered by the web. - To this point we need to have a professional website, dynamic and interactive where all users of your niche market interested in your services, goods and products; They can find you, know you and know more about you. - To achieve maximum success in this part of the positioning process must use a clear dominance that reflects your goal example: www.líderesconactitud.com. - finally, you need a design that is attractive and persuasive while motivate THE CALL TO ACTION users,

G. **Position yourself IN SOCIAL NETWORKS**: *Channels* Social Media important where you should be present can be Facebook, Twitter, YouTube, Google+, LinkedIn, Instagram, you should also keep up on blogs in your niche, this allows you to comment and answer questions. - These social networks represent a space in which to express all that other means cannot reflect. Additionally, search engines like Google highly value the top of the results when running a simple search. The basic tools you need to start your personal brand ONLINE are: A blog with your own domain name and a profile and fan page on Facebook. - The blog is important because it is where they're going to start talking about you and what you can do for a specific group of people interested in your niche, your blog will fulfill the role of virtual office of your business as it will be the ideal place for people to get to know more about you, you may want your blog have an autoresponder system built to start creating your list of prospects, subscribers and customers online. - FACEBOOK PROFILE You need to socialize, make yourself known, share posts on your wall and photos that inspire and motivate your friends and let them know the kind of person you are. "A good image and a good comment on your wall tells a thousand words" - Here the principle that applies very well. - In Facebook this applies much as a person to get to your profile can see the photographs and publications you have on your wall and know who you are, your interests, causes with which you identify, finally, your profile is a virtual representation of you. - You PAGE FANPAGE you do to satisfy your audience, people who are following your fan page is because they want to learn more of what you share and what you can do for them. - In your fan page can also give you a taste of what they can find on your blog, in other words, you fanpage page will be the vehicle to carry your followers to your blogger. - Whatever you decide to use social network Here are some tips to consider: 1. You must have clear objective, to know the whys and wherefores participate in the social network in question. 2nd Includes a real profile photo, and cover photo that reflects your professional goals. This transmit confidence and credibility in users operating in your social networks. - Complete 3rd full profile information, always being honest. By filling this information, you have the opportunity to introduce and publicize, your tastes, knowledge, achievements and preferences. - 4th Share content intelligently interest to your niche market constantly and permanently, this will keep you active in your followers. - 5th Make things happen, be proactive, take action. Ie take the lead, when you have your user's interactions with some of your posts or photos, this will make you consolidate relationships with your prospects, customers and prospects. - 4th Share content intelligently interest to your niche market constantly and permanently, this will keep you active in your followers. - 5th Make things happen, be proactive, take action. Ie take the lead, when you have your user's interactions with some of your posts or photos, this will make you consolidate relationships with your prospects, customers and prospects. - 4th Share content intelligently interest to your niche market constantly and permanently, this will keep you active in your followers. - 5th Make things happen, be proactive, take action. Ie take the lead, when you have your user's interactions with some of your posts or photos, this will make you consolidate relationships with your prospects, customers and prospects.

SUCCESS IS FOR THOSE THAT WE ARE WILLING TO PAY THE PRICE AND ENJOY THE ROAD "Success is more than one condition is a state of mind. Success is a journey; It is the consecutive achievement of small goals, and is the result of a life with purpose. And so, our goals are carried out; We must be willing to set our minds toward our destination, take action, implement the plan or project life and make things happen. " -. YLICH TARAZONA. -

---

Tips for positioning your personal brand strategies in person OFFLINE

*Consolidate and Position your PERSONAL BRANDING on a
Competitive Market Through "Love Brand"*

Written by Master Coach: YLICH TARAZONA

Well champions and champions as we have learned so far to create and build your personal brand or personal branding is a process that must begin to perform, if you really want to position yourself as a public image KNOWN.

With the issues we have developed so far, the importance of the Internet as online virtual tools is clear to build your personal brand IMAGE and publicize your business idea, goods, innovative product or service. We also learned the importance of applying the "LOVE BRAND" which is the ability to develop a personal brand, which produces the unconditional passion that people feel for their singers and actresses. The key "Love Brand" is in making a good first impression from the start. And produce empathy and rapport with the people with whom we interact daily. Whether such presence or virtual. And finally, we understood the importance of position and consolidate our PERSONAL BRANDING through physical actions and classroom activities known in the trade as MARKETING OFFLINE.

Then I will share with you another series of tips vital to start promoting your brand and personal or PERSONAL BRANDING through the REAL WORLD, known as OFFLINE.

Well without further ado let's begin ... =)

- *Begin to position ourselves as an expert through mini Courses and workshops.* - Another effective way to build your personal brand and position OFFLINE is attending meetings, social events, presentations and networking free activities. I can say that the first impression in person MARKETING CLASSROOM is the most effective way to build a fruitful relationship for the future. And for this to happen we must contribute to society and create opportunity for us to meet new people and above all so that they too can meet you. As we have repeatedly reaffirmed online resources (websites, blogs, social networks, tele seminars, webinars and podcasters) are very useful,

- *Heads up is also vital to our positioning as an image of personal brand, for this reason; we must walk the extra mile, go further, take action, make things happen, talk to as many people as possible, make presentations 1 to 1 (one to one), visit potential clients and prospects regularly exchange information. Such acts foster relationships and strengthen ties of amity. You never lose touch with friends, family, acquaintances and former colleagues or studies.*

- **She becomes an expert in traditional print publishing information and a speaker on radio and television presentations**. *A principle of excellence in successful people is getting known both written and spoken form; ie, you have to start trying to get a print and radio space to win your audience and wound as many people as possible in your niche. To start you can start from local newspapers, remember that local newspapers are in almost every city, local print and daily newspapers still have many readers and is an excellent choice to win readers in your field of action, given this possibility you can give known as a writer; You can start writing such an opinion about your niche giving options, alternatives and answers to your readers the subject of interest selected beforehand. - The other recommended option is radio and local television, radio stations and television programs also still have a large audience, it would be ideal to attend as a guest on radio or television, this will give the opportunity to make yourself known as an expert and find many interested audiences in goods, services or products you offer. - and if it is in your possibilities moderator and host of your own television program or the producer and host of your radio show would be great.*

Consolidate and Position your PERSONAL BRANDING on a Competitive Market Through "Love Brand"

Written by Master Coach: YLICH TARAZONA

- **Being part of something bigger** It is part of a global vision, get involved in organizations related to your ideals, entrepreneurial team member, an active part of a group of multilevel entrepreneurs; Mostly these businesses network marketing have an educational system and a support team that you can leverage to meet new friends and socialize with people and leaders who can teach you many things, participate in volunteer services, if you serve others, serve others will produce a double satisfaction, first, to help others, and then get good people to meet.

- **Invest in your health**; start taking care of your physical well-being, this may not seem as important as the above tips, but in truth it is, IMHO staff champions and champions believe that taking care of our physical appearance and our personal well-being is vital when start position our PERSONAL BRANDING. Remember you are the image of your personal brand is your business. For that reason; you should start taking care of your health, improve your eating habits, eat healthy and balanced way, you have to start practicing a sport which you feel more comfortable, for example, are aerobic exercises like "bailoterapia, spinning, yoga, pilate among others "are also anaerobic exercises such as" weights, machines multifuerzas "Anyway, this is just some ideas to keep in mind. Remember that the better you are; have greater impact among your fans and in the end, translates into greater confidence in yourself.

- Creates and develops "Love Brand". This is a good starting point in the positioning strategy and consolidate your personal brand IMAGE. It is time that your potential prospects, customers, partners and supporters become fans of your brand and "fall in love" your PERSONAL BRANDING. " inspire love for purposes of this principle is to make people feel excited toward what you offer, and feel great sympathy for what your image of personal brand represents for them." - How love our potential customers, prospects, partners and supporters. And turn them into fans of our personal brand through "Love Brand". - Remember to enter the minds and hearts of people, and make them become our best customers, prospects, partners and supporters, earning us their loyalty. It must be noted with a strategy of "Love Brand". To achieve this goal, it is necessary to create an emotional bond with them. Not enough that you try to do an excellent job and provide good service, you must learn to love what you do, and believe in what you do, be passionate with your work and fall in love with him as yourself. It is the only way to transmit the passion necessary to "reach the hearts and minds of potential customers, prospects, partners and supporters." And one of the ways is to involve people. Do it through its opinions, advice, recommendations, suggestions, let them let you know that you value what they think and feel. - However, to accomplish this task is essential to know well and identify your niche market, in order to be able to convey your brand as something you feel, and behave with them. Dare open up, and that people become part of you and what you do. Your customers, prospects, partners and supporters must become fans of your brand, they must have a sincere desire to recommend it spontaneously, provide feedback to other interested people. And to achieve this, we fear that make them feel they are part of our mission and vision. To do this, you must teach what are the values that govern your brand image PERSON and what are principles that underpin it. With these steps, not only will you win their respect and admiration, but more importantly, also their trust and loyalty. and that people become part of you and what you do. Your customers, prospects, partners and supporters must become fans of your brand, they must have a sincere desire to recommend it spontaneously, provide feedback to other interested people. And to achieve this, we fear that make them feel they are part of our mission and vision. To do this, you must teach what are the values that govern your brand image PERSON and what are principles that underpin it. With these steps, not only will you win their respect and admiration, but more importantly, also their trust and loyalty. and that people become part of you and what you do. Your customers, prospects, partners and supporters must become fans of your brand, they must have a sincere desire to recommend it spontaneously, provide feedback to other interested people. And to achieve this, we fear that make them feel they are part of our mission and vision. To do this, you must teach what are the values that govern your brand image PERSON and what are principles that underpin it. With these steps, not only will you win their respect and admiration, but more importantly, also their trust and loyalty. fear that make them feel they are part of our mission and vision. To do this, you must teach what are the values that govern your brand image PERSON and what are principles that underpin it. With these steps, not only will you win their respect and admiration, but more importantly, also their trust and loyalty. fear that make them feel they are part of our mission and vision. To do this, you must teach what are the values that govern your brand image PERSON and what are principles that underpin it. With these steps, not only will you win their respect and admiration, but more importantly, also their trust and loyalty.

- Create useful for your brand merchandising staff. The concept of merchandising applied to "{(PERSONAL BRANDING)}" is part of the online and offline marketing that covers business techniques to present to your potential customers and prospects the product or services you offer in the best possible conditions, either subjectively, persuasive, psychological, physical, tangible, palpable, visual, auditory or sensory as is the case of what we provide to our market niche interested in our specific area. - People are full of useless gifts that do not know what to do with them, affecting the corporate image they have of certain trademark. Although the budget for merchandising can produce a minimum investment spending in most cases, the most ideal first would think our potential clients and prospects and income that our gift will provide them. Our aim should be that the gift goes to do is to add value and benefit to those who receive it LIVE. - In this globalized world in which we live, it is one of the ERAS information, the virtual world and knowledge accelerated greater significance in recent years. - For this reason, we are persuaded to move at the same speed of the changes that are occurring in the market, demanding leaders, entrepreneurs and businessmen that we are positioning ourselves in the market to be part of that generational change. - Especially in these times when our prospects, customers, prospects, partners and supporters are looking increasingly to other colleagues in our own niche and specialty. - It is therefore; we must appeal more ethically and professionally your imagination to fall in love, to conquer and achieve win their trust and loyalty so they continue to believe in us and preferring products *and services we offer. - And the merchandising used properly is one of the best response option and alternative that exist for it ...*

How to create a strategy of "LOVE BRAND".

To achieve a strategy of "Love Brand" is a matter of applying certain tactics. To achieve this, we must establish strong bonds with people. To do this, I propose these 7 steps for "Love Brand" cash.

Love what you do. So that people love your brand, you must first begin to love yourself.

CREATE YOUR BRAND TO ATTRACT. To achieve this purpose, you must cause the interest of your potential customers, prospects, partners and supporters to the products or services you offer. To do this you can, use the power of stories, (Storytelling), creating a story or anecdote about your brand. (The STORYTELLING is to tell your story and make people connect with your words, and become an active part of your brand ... Through stories can stimulate the senses, desires and emotions of people and connect them more deeply with us.

Appeals to the senses. Personal branding, like the products, mainly enters the eyes, but also through other senses. If you get your PERSONAL BRANDING link to visual, auditory, kinesthetic and sensory stimuli, you've reached a level of unsurpassed bonding. (In practice, this translates to carefully choose your decorations, furniture, spaces, aromas, lighting, colors, shapes. Images and sounds ... I mean, use sensory marketing. What you see, hear, feel, taste and smells).

CARE SHOPPING EXPERIENCE. We have to win on the field of emotions, feelings and link us to memories of our client, because 95% of purchasing decisions are dictated by the unconscious. So, make sure you use the existential or experiential marketing. To put it into practice in your personal brand keep in mind these 4 keys: The experimental part (the pleasure of enjoying the product), part of entertainment (including elements linked to leisure and entertainment), the display portion (each product reaches the consumer in a very different way) and converting part (learn to share the qualities of the product, and shows how it's done or how to use it)

CREATE COMMUNITY. Much of the secret strategies "Love Brand" to position and strengthen your personal brand is the ability to make the customer feel that he is someone unique and exclusive part of a very special community. To do this, customize the most of your services or products, and give the opportunity to your customer, prospects, partners and fans to interact with you through your social networks such as blog, fanpage, chat, web surveys, among many other options. Use social media to reach them, and offer extra services as counseling, online and offline training, coachsulting and sections that can make virtual face as many as the niche market that you develop ...

TRANSMIT CONFIDENCE AND SECURITY. There is no "Love Brand" no confidence. It is not that we cannot make mistakes, but to accept them on time and recognize at the time when they occur. The key is, to convey confidence, and for that transparency, integrity and honesty are essential.

I KNOW SOLIDARITY. Practice generosity. In these times, it is good to be recognized for your service, for your solidarity and your willingness to help others.

Elements must have a good strategy "LOVE BRAND" for positioning and consolidate your brand.

"In addition to achieving high levels of empathy, love and loyalty of our customers, prospects and followers. A good strategy "Love Brand" must have a balanced manner the following elements: MYSTERY, sensory stimulation and passion.

MYSTERY: An image of personal brand must always retain some hidden mystery. In other words, keep your privacy reserved portion. For people to be attracted, and eager to learn more about you. The mystery increases the attraction for your brand, because people are attracted to the unknown.

Sensory stimulation: A good PERSONAL BRANDING, should Thenar the ability to stimulate the senses of people. Regardless of the niche market you're in, you must learn to encourage people visually, auditory, kinesthetic and sensuously through which you can make them see, feel and hear.

PASSION: Is drinks consist of the commitment of your strategy "Love Brand" to develop a true appreciation and sincere love for people. Babies learn to know your audience, create empathy and rapport with them, and you must always keep the passion for what you do and offer.

> "The training, preparation and attitude is the difference between success and failure." - YLICH TARAZONA. -

WORKBOOK

DETERMINE YOUR PLAN OF ACTION, positioning your personal brand

DEVELOP TACTICS AND STRATEGY

What is your niche? What AREA IN BOUQUET AND SPECIALTY going to develop to consolidate and establish your "{(personal brand)}" as an expert on the subject?

What is the main goal and purpose for which want to consolidate and establish your brand PERSONAL in the market?

Think of several tactics and strategies that will need to consolidate and position YOU "{(personal brand)}"

Think about people, partners, leaders or mentors who could help consolidate and establish your "personal brand} {"

What resources, skills and achieve accounts to achieve consolidate and establish your competence "{PERSONAL MARK}"?

What are some of the challenges to be overcome to achieve reach consolidate and establish your "personal brand {}"?

What social networks or web platform accounts to manage to reach consolidate and establish your "personal brand {}"?

What kind of events, activities, companies or similar organizations are going to start going to achieve reach and promote consolidate and establish your "personal brand {}"?

What recourse, skill or special skills you need to achieve consolidate and establish your "{(personal brand)}"? and How do you think you could get them to achieve your goals?

What evaluation measures you will take; to determine whether it is achieving consolidate and position YOU "{(personal brand)}"?

What are the tactics and strategies that are going to implement and use to consolidate and establish your personal brand in person, OFFLINE?

What are the tactics and strategies that are going to implement and use to consolidate and establish your brand PERSONAL virtually, ONLINE?

What tactics and strategies you will begin to use to start your process of "Love Brand" that allows you to consolidate and establish your "PERSONAL} {TRADEMARK" from the beginning?

Do you think about various tactics and strategies that you can use to incorporate your "Love Brand" as a means to consolidate and establish your "personal brand} {" As you go making known?

How will you carry out your "Love Brand" to conquer the heart of your niche market and consolidate and establish your "personal brand {}"?

Write like you then "Love Brand" will help consolidate and establish your "personal brand {}

Knowing where we are going, it is important and essential in our path to personal excellence, have a north set allows us to walk in the right direction, knowing where we allow us to set the path and the coordinates for which we must lead and guide us to reach our destination. In other words, we are clear about our mission in life and know what is the purpose that gives meaning to our existence, is what allows us to finally rediscover why we are here and we are born. Let us remember that we are all born with a purpose, we all have a mission and when we discover and we pursue it, this will not only give meaning to our existence, but open endless chances to take us straight to our destination.

-. *YLICH TARAZONA.* -

THE POWER OF ESTABLISHMENT AND DEFINITION OF GOALS FOR ACHIEVING GOALS "fully understand and clearly that is what they really want to achieve to achieve in every aspect of your life. Have well-defined goals and clear objectives and established step by step. This will prevent wasting time put in not knowing what to do or where to start. When you know why and with whom you share your triumphs, this will be put in place to implement its plan of action AS to get it. But above all will allow you to start focusing on the end result, focused on its vision and mission of purpose "

-. *YLICH TARAZONA.* -

FINAL WORDS

Good champions and champions "{(CONGRATULATIONS)}" because we have reached the end of this wonderful book in its special edition with such dedication that I wrote for you. It was a long process of training and learning together you and I rode on this journey to your success and personal fulfillment.

This book is created and designed with IT in mind, SYSTEMATICALLY as a PRACTICAL INSTRUCTION MANUAL step by step; with the aim of going through a mental process of continuous learning training, through a "{(PATTERN OF ACTION)}" well prepared and simplified to provide optimal, effective and permanent results through the tools and methodologies of NEUROLINGUISTICS PROGRAMMING

<u>SEE YOU IN THESE BOOKS SERIES ...</u>
"Basic Principles for Success and Introductory Success"

If you liked this book Positioning your personal brand and want to "help" with your contribution, to support me to continue doing this wonderful work, which, with love, prepared for you. I can make it through the following link

http://bit.ly/PaypalDonación
Thank you for your contribution

It's time to start living
WONDERFUL LIFE
Centered Principles

Remember, take action and
MAKE THINGS HAPPEN

And soon you and I will see us in the
CUSP OF EXCELLENCE

Your Great Friend *Ylich Tarazona*

MásterCoach.YlichTarazona@gmail.com
http://www.reingenieriamentalconpnl.com

Consolidate and Position your PERSONAL BRANDING on a Competitive Market Through "Love Brand"
Written by Master Coach: YLICH TARAZONA

ABOUT THE AUTHOR

PROFESSIONAL BACKGROUND:

Transformational Coach YLICH TARAZONA: Renowned writer, best-selling author, speaker and lecturer International High Level.

Expert in NLP or Neuro Linguistic Programming, Reengineering Brain, bioprogramming Mental, Neuro Coaching, Persuasion and Hypnosis.

Considered in various media as one of the most prominent and influential within the field of neuroscience and personal excellence MOTIVATIONAL Entrepreneurs; destined to have a legacy in the lives of thousands of people, through their passion, enthusiasm, dynamism and principle-centered leadership.

Man, of faith and Christian convictions; centered Principles and Values.

Reengineering founder MENTAL portal PNL ®- Virtual Community for Entrepreneurs. One of the Internet Website dedicated to providing COACHING in consolidating Skills and Development of Human Potential Maximum. Specialists in training, education and training of high level through neurolinguistics programming.

Creator PERSONAL COACHING SYSTEM Reengineering and bioprogramming MENTAL CEREBRAL to achieve goals, to define objectives and develop effective results optimal performance; through a series of audios, Podcasters, Tele-Seminars Online, Audio-Visual Workshops, Webinars and Conferences Master of attending classes.

Co-Creator and Re-designer of "NLP model" and effective formula "{(E - SMART - ER)}" [for the establishment and goal setting, action plan and principles of strategic planning to achieve and consolidate objectives].

Webminars creator Audio Visual, teleseminar Online and KEYNOTE [Re-Discovering Your Life Purpose and Mission].

Recognized "Author of the book series, sequences and EBOOK'S KEYNOTE" of [Reengineering CEREBRAL and bioprogramming MENTAL © -®]. Among the highlights we "As Improving Your Self-Esteem", "Liberate the Internal Self-Sabotage", "Rediséñate and Reinvent Your Life Position your personal brand or Personal Branding, Reengineering thought processes among others.

Consolidate and Position your PERSONAL BRANDING on a Competitive Market Through "Love Brand"

Written by Master Coach: YLICH TARAZONA

Best-selling author series [THE MASTERS OF CYCLES duplication and multiplication in the MARKETING NETWORKS Law and Universal Principles to Develop Your Business Multilevel professionally] Vol. 1, 2 and 3.

Creator of INTEGRAL SYSTEM PERSONAL COACHING through NLP or Neuro Linguistic Programming to produce positive changes in thought patterns, and generate effective results of high performance and optimal performance, both individual and organizational levels. Said TRAINING SYSTEM Offline and Online have marked the lives of hundreds of entrepreneurs in person and has changed the mental paradigms of thousands of people worldwide virtual path. Inspire participants, they hear, see or read his teachings; to live extraordinarily focused on principles.

MISSION AND PERSONAL VISION:

MY PURPOSE: Convey to all my readers faith; and the strength to move forward, always with confidence and optimism despite adversity. Guiding them as his mentor and coach staff find their life mission through a real opportunity for personal growth, to help them clarify their ideas, set goals, and develop a well-defined plan of action, enabling them to successfully conquer your wildest dreams. Allowing them to create their own future, writing the story of his own life and forging their own destiny through a continuous cycle of tactics and strategies created for that purpose.

Similarly, I want to help my readers, trainees, participants and supporters to change negative thought patterns and limiting mindsets, teaching them to consolidate their skills and develop their maximum human potential.

MY MISSION: Becoming an instrument in God's hands, that allows me to impact the lives of hundreds, thousands and millions of people around the world.

Leave a mark that makes a difference in the lives of the people I teach and carry my message. And also leave them a legacy that transcends time. And let them evolve in all transcendental and important aspects of their lives, both personally, spiritually, emotionally as well as professionally, academically and financially.

MY VISION: Bringing people hope and an option that allows them to transform their lives for the better, to help them develop that seed of greatness we all carry within its interior, and encourage them to consolidate position and expand their maximum human potential, next level of success.

And finally, to establish a connection and empathy with all my readers, participants and supporters, to let me go climbing in the relationship with each of them, as far as possible. At the same time, I teach them to position and consolidate in all aspects of life in a balanced way ...

Helping them internalize the correct principles that allow them to reinvent itself, creating a new and improved version of themselves. Opening up new paths, new opportunities aperturandoles success, enabling them to lead their lives, to find himself on the road to transformation and personal excellence. And finally; resume more strongly, his path to success and personal excellence ...

*Consolidate and Position your PERSONAL BRANDING on a
Competitive Market Through "Love Brand"*
Written by Master Coach: YLICH TARAZONA

OTHER PUBLICATIONS, SPECIAL EDITIONS, MINI COURSES, BOOKS BY THE AUTHOR

Hello such, my great friend and friend reader, was a pleasure to have shared with you this time reading, I hope you enjoyed the most of the information in this book so lovingly prepared for you.

If you want to know some other of my works on Kindle from Amazon and CreateSpace I invite you to visit the following links. you great friend goodbye Coach YLICH TARAZONA

1.- HOW TO IMPROVE YOUR SELF-ESTEEM. *Learn to program your mind and focus your thoughts to conquer everything that you propose in Life.*
Amazon Kindle https://www.amazon.com/dp/B071NS4NPH
Paperback CreateSpace https://www.createspace.com/6763814

2.- *Liberate the self-sabotaging.* **Learn to Strengthen Your Inner Warrior, Energy Balance your channels, control your emotions and direct your thoughts.**
Amazon Kindle https://www.amazon.com/dp/B0716BWKR1
Paperback CreateSpace https://www.createspace.com/7120751

3.- *REDISÉÑATE and re YOUR LIFE.* **The Art REDESIGN your life, REINVENT, BE REBORN and create a new and improved version of yourself.**
Amazon Kindle https://www.amazon.com/dp/B06XKCSTNZ
Paperback CreateSpace https://www.createspace.com/7195297

4.- *REDISCOVERING your life purpose.* **Foundations for Living a Full Life, principle-centered and connected with Our Vision and Mission.**
Amazon Kindle https://www.amazon.com/dp/B071FFVVM4
Paperback CreateSpace https://www.createspace.com/7195692

5.- THE POWER OF GOALS. *Principles of Strategic Planning to achieve and consolidate your dreams and goals step by step.*
Amazon Kindle https://www.amazon.com/dp/B071SF2QX7
Paperback CreateSpace https://www.createspace.com/6684686

6.- POSITIONING YOUR BRAND PERSON. *Consolidate and establish your PERSONAL BRANDING in a competitive market through the "Love Brand".*
Amazon Kindle https://www.createspace.com/6799772
Paperback CreateSpace https://www.createspace.com/6615804

Written by Master Coach: YLICH TARAZONA

7.- *NEURO-LINGUISTIC PROGRAMMING. Practical Guide PNL COMPLETED - Modern Methodologies and Techniques for Effective Change Your Life*.
Kindle Amazon https://www.amazon.com/dp/B072DVXBHR
Paperback CreateSpace https://www.createspace.com/7119256

8.- *The power of metaphors and figurative language. Stories, parables, metaphors and allegories, Powerful Persuasive Communication Tools*.
Amazon Kindle https://www.amazon.com/dp/B01ESBD7WY
Paperback CreateSpace https://www.createspace.com/6685297

9.- *Reengineering CEREBRAL AND REDESIGN OF THOUGHT. Learn to reprogram Your Mental Processes and generate a Personal Reinvention*.
Amazon Kindle https://www.amazon.com/dp/B0723BVN9G
Paperback CreateSpace https://www.createspace.com/6685293

10-. *THE POWER OF HYPNOSIS. Theoretical and Practical Manual Training HYPNOSIS and Skills Development Hypnotic Persuasive*.
Amazon Kindle https://www.amazon.com/dp/B076G97F14
Paperback CreateSpace https://www.createspace.com/7691037

eleven-. *PRACTICAL COURSE OF HYPNOSIS. How to hypnotize, anyone, Anytime, Anywhere*.
Amazon Kindle https://www.amazon.com/dp/B076G97F14
Paperback CreateSpace https://www.createspace.com/7691037

12-. *HYPNOSIS TO THE NEXT LEVEL. Advanced hypnotism, self-hypnosis, regression and Hypnotic Phenomena High Level*.
Amazon Kindle https://www.amazon.com/dp/B076G97F14
Paperback CreateSpace https://www.createspace.com/7691037
Coming soon...

13-. *THE BIG BOOK OF HYPNOSIS. Hypnotism manual to learn hypnotize Anyone, Anytime, Anywhere*.
Amazon Kindle https://www.amazon.com/dp/B076G97F14
Paperback CreateSpace https://www.createspace.com/7691037
Coming soon...

14.- *Multilevel marketing networks. Masters Cycles of duplication and multiplication in the Network Marketing*.
Amazon Kindle https://www.amazon.com/dp/B01IZTHD0M
Paperback CreateSpace https://www.createspace.com/6614144

15.- PLANNING BUSINESS NOTEBOOK. *Monthly Action Plan to Develop Your Business Successfully Multilevel professionally.*
Amazon Kindle https://www.amazon.com/dp/B01J1JEVHI
Paperback CreateSpace https://www.createspace.com/6612779

16.- NETWORK MARKETING TO THE NEXT LEVEL. *Universal principles to develop your MLM Project Successfully professionally.*
Amazon Kindle https://www.amazon.com/dp/B01MFDJNT9
Paperback CreateSpace https://www.createspace.com/6619923

17.- MULTILEVEL MARKETING NETWORK. *Network Marketing Business Opportunity Great XXI Century, Towards your financial freedom.*
Amazon Kindle https://www.amazon.com/dp/B01M5H4CG2
Paperback CreateSpace https://www.createspace.com/6669735

18. WORDS AND PHRASES FAMOUS INSPIRATIONAL. *Collection with more than 800 Thoughts and motivational quotes Leaders Largest in History.*
Amazon Kindle https://www.amazon.com/dp/B01J4MGSU0
Paperback CreateSpace https://www.createspace.com/6615169

19.- *PNL applied to communication.* *Patterns Persuasion, Conversational Hypnosis and Hypnotic Oratory, the Art of Persuasion, and Influence Others Positively.*
Amazon Kindle https://www.amazon.com/dp/B01MXT273E
Paperback CreateSpace https://www.createspace.com/6762851
Coming soon...

20.- THE ART OF COACHING WITH NLP. *Knowledge, Skills, Techniques, Coaching Practices and Strategies to achieve goals and achieve what thou meanest in the Living.*
Amazon Kindle https://www.amazon.com/dp/B01N1N49V8
Paperback CreateSpace https://www.createspace.com/6762787
Coming soon...

21.- *Reengineering MENTAL CEREBRAL and programming.* *A quantum leap in the evolution of SER - The New Era of Thought and The Awakening of Consciousness.*
Amazon Kindle https://www.amazon.com/dp/B01EQML2U4
Paperback CreateSpace https://tsw.createspace.com/6685305
Coming soon...

Consolidate and Position your PERSONAL BRANDING on a Competitive Market Through "Love Brand"
Written by Master Coach: YLICH TARAZONA

22.- LAW AND UNIVERSAL PRINCIPLES OF SUCCESS. Biblical Principles for Success and Abundance Living in accordance with the Lord's Way.
Amazon Kindle https://www.amazon.com/dp/B01MQQWLGT
Softcover CreateSpace https://www.createspace.com/6762826
Coming soon...

To acquire other PRESENTATION OPTIONS and I acquired the BOOKS in versions STANDARD SOFT COVER or PREMIUM, PROFESSIONAL HARD COVER WITH or WITHOUT COVER, WITH or WITHOUT BACK COVER, in different qualities of prints (Black and White, Full Color, Premium Bonded Sheet) in Size Pocket, American Printing or Spiral ...

You can make them through my other OFFICIAL Portals.

http://www.lulu.com/spotlight/Coach_YlichTarazona
http://www.autoreseditores.com/coach.ylich.tarazona

Constant learning, continuous training and ongoing study are the keys among those who achieve success, those who do not. - Ylich Tarazona. -

PUBLICATIONS, EDITIONS, BOOKS, AND SPECIAL REPORTS CREATED BY THE AUTHOR

*Consolidate and Position your PERSONAL BRANDING on a
Competitive Market Through "Love Brand"*
Written by Master Coach: YLICH TARAZONA

OTHER PUBLICATIONS, EDITIONS, BOOKS, AND SPECIAL REPORTS CREATED BY THE AUTHOR

CONTINUATION OF THE SERIES

WORKSHOPS, CONFERENCES, SEMINARS, MINI COURSES CREATED BY THE AUTHOR

*Consolidate and Position your PERSONAL BRANDING on a
Competitive Market Through "Love Brand"*
Written by Master Coach: YLICH TARAZONA

AUDIO BOOKS, PODCASTS, WEBINARS, AND VIDEOS CREATED BY THE AUTHOR

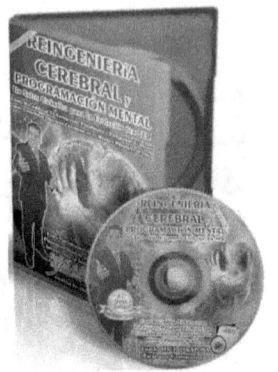

FOLLOW US THROUGH ALL OUR SOCIAL NETWORKS (SOCIAL MEDIA AND OFFICIAL WEBSITE)

Facebook, Twitter, YouTube, Google +, BlogSpot, Instagram, Pinterest, SlideShare, Speaker, LinkedIn, Skype y Gmail

https://www.amazon.com/Ylich-Eduard-Tarazona-Gil/e/B01INP4SU6
http://www.reingenieriamentalconpnl.com/
http://www.coachylichtarazona.com/

http://www.lulu.com/spotlight/Coach_YlichTarazona

http://www.autoreseditores.com/coach.ylich.tarazona

https://www.facebook.com/coachmaster.ylichtarazona

https://www.youtube.com/user/coachylichtarazona

https://plus.google.com/+ylichtarazona/posts

http://www.spreaker.com/user/ylich_tarazona

http://instagram.com/coach_ylich_tarazona/

https://www.pinterest.com/ylich_tarazona/

https://www.linkedin.com/in/ylichtarazona

http://es.slideshare.net/ylichtarazona

https://twitter.com/ylichtarazona

You can also contact the AUTHOR directly via e-mail by:
MasterCoach.YlichTarazona@gmail.com

Skype: Coaching_Empresarial

Consolidate and Position your PERSONAL BRANDING on a
Competitive Market Through "Love Brand"
Written by Master Coach: YLICH TARAZONA

3rd Special Edition *Revised and Updated by:* ***Ylich Tarazona*** *October 2017.*
Design and Preparation of the Cover by: Ylich Tarazona

ISBN-13: **978-1979861687** *(CreateSpace-Assigned)*
ISBN-10: **1979861684** *(CreateSpace-Assigned)*
STAMP: Independently Published ©

BISAC: Personal Brand / Personal Branding / Love Brand / Entrepreneurship
The right of **YLICH TARAZONA** *to be identified as the* **AUTHOR** *of this work has been affirmed by SafeCreative.org, Registration Code:* **1711184869558***, in accordance with* **Copyright Worldwide***. Date:* **November 17, 2017***.*

www.ingramcontent.com/pod-product-compliance
Lightning Source LLC
Chambersburg PA
CBHW050023230526
45470CB00003B/1103